D0515112

where river meets ocean

devorah major

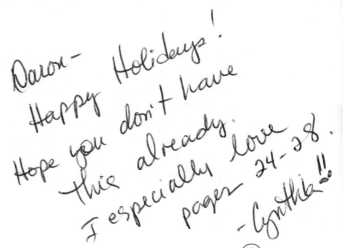

Daron—
Happy Holidays!
Hope you don't have
this already.
I especially love
pages 24–38.
—Cynthia!!

POET LAUREATE SERIES NUMBER ③

CITY LIGHTS FOUNDATION
San Francisco

Copyright © 2003 by devorah major
All Rights Reserved
10 9 8 7 6 5 4 3 2 1

Cover photograph: devorah major at the Martin Luther King, Jr. fountain in
Yerba Buena Center
by David T. Pang, courtesy of *Tea Party Magazine*
Cover design & typography: Yolanda Montijo

Library of Congress Cataloging-in-Publication Data
Major, Devorah, 1952–
  Where river meets ocean / Devorah Major.
     p.cm.-- (Poet laureate series ; no.3)
   ISBN 1-931404-03-8 (alk.paper)
   1. San Francisco (Calif.)—Poetry. I.Title. II. Poet
laureate series (City Lights Foundation) ; no. 3.
   PS3563.A3915W48   2003
   811'.
54—dc21   2003053197

CITY LIGHTS FOUNDATION
publications are edited by Lawrence Ferlinghetti and
Nancy J. Peters and published at the City Lights
Bookstore, 261 Columbus Ave, San Francisco CA 94133
www.citylights.com

ACKNOWLEDGMENTS

City Lights Foundation gratefully acknowledges the following publications and performances of some of the poems in this volume:

"downtown" was published in *With More Than Tongue* (Creative Arts Books, 2000)

"fillmore street woman" and "kapow" were published in *Street Smarts* (Curbstone Press, 1996)

"terrorism defined" was published in *An Eye for an Eye Makes the Whole World Blind: Poets on 911* (Regent Press, 2002)

"black lit class and ellison's invisible man" and "first person singular" were published in *Obsidian III Literature in the African Diaspora*, vol. 1, number 1, 1999

"tendered love" was published in *The African American Pulpit: Millenium*, Issue 2002

"privacy" was published in *The New Progressive Magazine*, November 1998

"a cuba song" and "in answer" were originally written for and performed in Si Como No, an Afro-Cuban jazz dance theatrical.

TABLE OF CONTENTS

INAUGURAL ADDRESS

Poetry makes me smile. Even when it makes me cry, even when its bite sends chills up my spine, even when it howls its hot ice fury, if it speaks truth, it warms me up inside, and a part of me smiles. I love poetry. Poetry, with its infinite rhythms and shadings, wears robes in so many colors and fabrics that you can travel the world in its grasp, ride through its bazaar of tastes and tongues as it speaks its languages of love, of struggle, of determination, of faith, of our humanity and our universes. I love poetry because it is a warrior for truth and passion that takes no prisoners, only converts. For me, the best of poetry is like jazz in its ability to have people who don't always speak the same language swinging to the same beat. And if you want to swing to the world in poetry, San Francisco is probably one of the better places to be. In San Francisco you can be at home and traverse the planet at the same time.

San Francisco has held poets and poetry from its beginning. First, were the Ohlone, who traded on its beaches with the nearby Miwok not only baskets, fish, and deer skins but also song, verse, and stories, all fed by the drum. Much of that voice was silenced as first conquistadors and then, years later, pioneers began to create settlements that soon became cities. Then the earth that held the healing bushes, the yerba buena that grew wild on this land, was turned to San Francisco. But now the city is once again home to many representatives of Indian nations, and their poets' voices grow strong again in images like San Francisco-based Tsalagi/Sauk and Fox poet Kim Shuck's creek in a storm:

> *I forgot to ask for the name*
> *Of the creek that used to run through*
> *What is now my backyard.*
> *They piped it under,*
> *But with enough rain*
> *It remembers where to go*

San Francisco has always been a fertile ground for poets. Forty-niners brought poetry with their pickaxes and saddlebags. African Americans in the 1850s were writing poems and creating hymns, publishing them in their newspapers, performing them in their cultural club, in their churches. The Chinese carved their poems in graceful calligraphy on Angel Island jail walls, and then those who finally found a home in our chopstick alleys continued to write, first in their native tongues and later in English. This area, this city, has always been a place where cultures crossed paths.

Some neighborhoods have, of course, stood out as areas where poets congregated and sharpened their craft. North Beach, for example, resonates poems, not just as historical monuments to the Beats, but as life force. If you happen there you will find vital poetry, of course in Ferlinghetti's venerable City Lights Bookstore, but also in the cafés, in the clubs, sometimes on the street corners. If you are particularly lucky you might happen on Jack Hirschman sharing poems, perhaps his own or maybe one of his translations from French or Albanian, from Haitian Creole or Italian, or from one of the other polyglot of tongues in which he writes and lives. Perhaps it will be a poem he wrote that morning, or the night before, but whenever its creation, it will be of the now, and however international its tongue, it will come close to home, crying for justice, for, as he writes:

our home, our land
Homeland once and for all
for one and all
and not just this one-legged cry
on a crutch on a rainy sidewalk.

I grew up in the shadow of North Beach's Bob Kaufman, devoured *Golden Sardine* and *Solitudes Crowded With Loneliness* as if I had never heard a poem before. He wrote:

The first man was an idealist, but he died,
he couldn't survive the first truth,
discovering that the whole
world, all of it, was all his, he sat down

& with a piece of string, & a sharp stone
invented suicide.

You see, the poetry of San Francisco that I am talking about is not a poetry that is simply folded between the covers of a book, pages still crisp after years on a shelf. The poetry that I speak of is a poetics that comes through, and is for, the people. A street-corner poetry, a café poetry, an on-the-bus poetry, an in-our-parks poetry, an in-your-face poetry. A poetry for the many, asking hard questions, posing alternate visions, showing us not only the city, or the nation, or even the planet, but the layers of the universe where we live, a multitude of the shades of the humanity that we defile or embrace, scorn or love.

I was about nineteen years old when I first heard a poem by a Vietnamese poet. It was a translation from a book of poetry by Ho Chi Min. Several of us were crammed inside a car rolling through Fillmore, all of us proudly black, as one of the sisters turned to the back of the car and read from a slim volume she had just discovered. Sometimes someone commented on a particular verse, sometimes we all just nodded and affirmed as she went on to find another and read that one, too. *"After winter comes spring, what could be more natural,"* she read, repeating the poem's last lines a few times. And then we all repeated them a few times until, moments later, we reached our destination, changed in almost imperceptible, but yet persistent, ways by the poem.

I like the way poetry shows up like that, represents in unlikely places, is at home anywhere, if its rhythm is true and its heart open. Tonight some Vietnamese poets are gathering with their community and reading their poems because April 30th is the twenty-seventh anniversary of the end of the Vietnam War. They are celebrating and mourning and remembering, and they are being a part of the San Francisco poetry world. Perhaps Saigon-born MöngLan is reading about the world seen now from San Francisco where

the Golden Gate Bridge from my window

> *is a red of smothered crabs*
> *cooked in dreamfog*

Tonight in the Mission, too, poets are holding forth. There, the poetry is like the anise Juan Felipe Herrera speaks of as

It roams
emitting its vapor . . .

writing its vengeance on walls . . .

tossing
its idea
into the random alleys.

You see, San Francisco is, as a local poetry organization asserts in its name, A City of Poets. Just up the hill from my Western Addition home Genny Lim lives and sculpts her poems, mixing her words with poetry and jazz, caring as much, if not more, for poetry as performance on air than embedded on pages, bringing China and Chinatown to her universal view:

got the transcontinental railroad tattooed on my back
Twenty thousand pounds of bones bound for China
Home is here, where the heart beats
Where the ghost of Anna May Wong and Jimmy Wong Howe sleeps

Every community and every age make poetry in San Francisco. So many people, so many corners, that the more I name, the more I quote, the more I am forced to leave out. There are so many good poets who speak from their cultures, in their languages, with the music that is unique to their clan, yet is also verse that is star and cosmos in the sensibilities of us all. Indeed I have not named any poets of the Sunset, the Richmond, Bernal Heights, Excelsior, but they are there holding forth, with strength and eloquence. And I have omitted so many poetry communities with skilled, dynamic voices—Filipinos, Irish, East Indians, Palestinians. And I have not even made mention of the poetry schools, some of which have barricades and weapons poised, the new formalists, the spoken word MCs, the traditionalists. Or the youth or the elders or the disabled. You see, it is all in San Francisco.

I must tell you I find it strange to be a poet making a speech. You see, the work that brought me here is inside the poems. It lives as breath and rain, not as narrative exclaiming or proclaiming. And it is as poet, not speechmaker, that I intend to fill the post of poet laureate. I will continue to write poems of and for the city, a city that has schooled me, embraced me, fed me, a city that now honors me. But it is not always easy to write about San Francisco.

It is easy to praise its beauty. Even on a dank, slate-gray day when the fog washes everything with sharp nails that cut through any space in your garb, even as it presses ice needles into your bones, even then San Francisco's hills still roll, Golden Gate Park still blossoms in rainbows of green, the bay still beckons, and a group of swimmers, who seem to trace their symbolic genealogies back to Icelandic sagas, slice through Aquatic Park beach waves.

It is easy to praise the poets of San Francisco. Any day, any night there is an opportunity to hear poetry, to live poetry. No, not every poet is worth hearing. No, not every poem has magic. But at each of the cafés or clubs, libraries or schools or community organizations around the city, one or more poets are moving forward, perhaps with paper trembling in hand, perhaps unsure how to approach the mike, perhaps commandingly raising their voices over the cash register and customers, perhaps with rhymes undulating off their tongues; perhaps shooting fire, or spilling sweat, but surely breaking open the moment with the madness and the majesty of spirit in word.

But San Francisco is not only a city to be glorified and praised, a tourist gemstone at the center of strings of memorable odes and romantic ballads. Perhaps the hardest part of being a poet, not just here but anywhere, and perhaps one of the more important parts of being a poet, is to look in the corners that are not so wonderful, to find poetry in the blemishes and the stains.

For example, when I am downtown I always hear the voices, see the faces, feel the mantra that sweeps this wealthy nation's streets:

spare change   spare a quarter   hungry
got a quarter   spare any change   hungry
need a quarter need a quarter   hungry
spare change   hungry
do you have any   need a quarter

across one block
hands, empty cups, hats
stretch in front of our
spiked heels, scuffed broughams,

high-tech rubber soles
dyed hair and toupees
leather bags
see-through plastic bags
neon-orange bags
monogrammed paper bags
hurrying to the corner to wait
talking loudly
sometimes to ourselves
stepping past the curbs and doorways
where they stoop and stand

one does not have calves or feet
can you spare any
another has on an army jacket
hungry
a third shivers

under woolen overcoat
in the heat of August

most are men
some are children   *need a quarter*
most are white or black   *spare change*
young enough to have family friends babies
do you have any
old enough to know another way to live
spare change   hungry
spare a quarter   need
do you

I came to adulthood in the Western Addition, honed my own poetry at Minnie's Can-Do Club on Fillmore: beer, wine, pool table, regular people. I still live in that part of the city, but with all the changes, sometimes those streets seems like strangers. Sometimes the black community that made its first inroads there over a hundred and fifty years ago seems to be the interloper.

she is a dark woman
treading water
in a life of hard choices.
wrong decisions
limited alternatives
stock-pens are embedded
in her eyes and mouth.

once she knew she was beautiful.

if you look closely
you can still feel
the edges of the fire that burned
in her eyes, on her skin
in the way her back arched
across fillmo'e street corners.

she wore her nails
sculpted in red
in those days
when that street
when this street
was ours

she sat on a barstool
snapped her fingers
and hunched her shoulders
as smoke rose between
the bandstand and counter
and the scene
got hot and sultry
and the music
pressed out the doors
and down the street.

further down
she slid in at jack's
had another cigarette lit,
flashed her teeth, laughed
as the club spun tight
shoulder to shoulder
thick smoke and blaring saxophone.

then she checked in with minnie,
bought a pitcher of beer and half-way
listened to some crazy poets
chant a continent of promises
with congo drum and shakere
punctuating the rhythms
and a flute solo
bursting out over
the tastiest of love poems

maybe, maybe
she slipped into connie's
for some curried goat and coconut bread
or sweated spices next door
as leonard pulled another
sweet potato pie
out the oven and poured
his brown-red biting sauce
over smoking tender ribs
telling stories

as she savored another mouthful
then, when the street was ours.

she can see those days.
she knows them.
she remembers
before, before
imported cheese
before brandy-filled truffles
before double lattes
hand-made paper cards.
she sits on the iron-rimmed
privately owned bench
to rest her feet
and take the pinch
out of her back.
she holds the bitter in her mouth
sometimes spits it out at passerby
with steel in her stare
there on that bench
on that corner
on that block
on that street
that was ours, that was hers
that was taken, that we let go
that is lost, that was fillmo'e
when the streets held the people
and the musicians had names

and the rhythm was blues
and the downbeat was jazz
and the color
was black and fierce
like her.

At night I often find myself in front of my glowing computer screen typing away or watching solitaire card bytes shuffle and reshuffle themselves when the words won't wake up. Too often the stillness of the moment is broken by the sounds of gunfire outside my window.

listen
to the buzz
humming
around words
ping
pow
zap
kapow
tat tat rat a tat tat

place your
ear against the ground
next to the ringing water pipes
still your sighs
breathe in silence
stand in waiting

around the syllables
zap
pow
ping kapow
zip tat rat tat tat rat ta tat tat
as you listen
an earthquake tremor
becomes a four-hundred-year fall
off the richter scale
into a cascade of automatic rifles
recycled saturday night specials
two-bit twenty-twos
playing to a dying house
kapow, zap, rat tat tat
bam, bam bam bam
and then the gasp,
whine
shudder
thud.

last night bullets
rang again
wild west
live on tv .
news at eleven
popping hollow and thin.
gunfire explodes against the night
flashes like a blaring series

of freeway headlights
caught in your rear view mirror
squeezing blood into your brain.
they pop against night.

beirut some say.
it has become a metaphor
so much easier
to deal with than reality
down under, right over
there
the need not to look at
inner city outer limits.

not simply a burst
a new year's debacle
a fourth of july surrender
but a rhythm
a nightly beat of armaments
pointed at self
hip hop ranting rhythms
with a bass uzi coming in
and shaking windows
on the downbeat swing.

beirut some call it as a metaphor
only it's home, the blocks
where bloods sharpen

fewer and simpler words
fuck meaning fuck
chill reaching beyond iceboxes
and motherfucker meaning more than the dozens.

they play wild west at night
when dawn should be
caressed and assuaged
when lovers should turn and
stoke each other's backs
enjoy the crevices
between
thigh/groin/tongue/cheek
when babies should
suckle their mother's breast
greedy for its butterfat
when old people need only
listen to their knees and elbows
creak while considering if getting up
is worth all the angle-sharp pangs
of inevitable aging,
but instead
the night begins its symphony
ping pop zip click
pop pop double pop
zap
chchchchccch
bullets burst as bubblegum balloons

around our houses and our dreams.

again tonight, and again and again
and the news calls it
somewhere across the planet
somewhere you don't live
but it's here too
in your city
in your country
on your turf

close to each day's dawning
bullets converse
against a soon-to-be-gray sky.
they chatter amidst
the plasterboard walls
and every dawn
no matter what battles
have been fought and lost
every dawn
birds come and sing
perched in the wounded trees
kapow
pop pop
double pop zap
in silent surrender they roost
as the children
play wild wild west for real

pop pop double zing zap
kapow

Because there is this other San Francisco, this difficult San Francisco, this San Francisco that nurtures, but also sometimes swallows its young whole, I will be using part of my tenure as poet laureate to create bridges that will provide public poetry dialogues between the generations and neighborhoods, about what is happening on their streets, to their age-mates, to them. I am hoping to work with Youth Speaks, the San Francisco Public Libraries, and City of Poets to ask people to write and, in a living memorial, to present poems that examine the sadness and miracles, the love and destruction that are a part of this city. Poems that reach out to, echo, support, and reflect other cities, other nations, and other peoples' struggles and triumphs. San Francisco, peninsula though it is, is linked by more than bridges to the East and the North. It is attached by more than land to the South; it is bound by more than history to the rest of the nation. It is a microcosm in more than metaphor of the wars and truces, the terrors and struggles, the yearnings for peace and love that are a part of people all over this planet.

Poetry, you see, can be a force that helps us see, and if we see clearly we can move in the right direction. Poetry can be a force that makes us feel, can help us to know one another, and in that knowing to move righteously through our love.

these times are
more than dangerous

what is there but blood
blood and death
hunger
hunger and fear

starvation of body and spirit
a cruelty cut deep
into the maelstrom of our lives

the hour is late
and we must
rise up
resist
build barricades
and armories
and yet all i can
add to the stockpile
is a home-made
pocket-size acorn-
tool of a solution
a portion of my love
not enough i know
i wish i could offer you more

more than a steamy caress
i want to give something
that will ease the chaos

reduce the misery
foment a cure
and all i have is love
an open-handed love
a never empty rice-pot of love
a love garden that even in
winter bears fruit and flower

in this place of humanity
cordoned off
stripped
caged
forgotten in rich men's dreams
of star wars and
capitalistic metaphysical
pornographic fantasies
where all is owned
and everyone
and everything
has a price
even god

i have nothing to offer
but love
love and outrage

i hide my despair
fight daily against

a brine of hate that will curdle
my spirit and clog my will
push it back and offer love

one cannot fight a revolution
with such a paltry weapon
even a wordsmith must have more
i would become the red of the lava
spewed from the volcano's stomach
spurt and flow and in my wake
coax a few flowers to grow

here i stand with nothing
but my hands
and my eyes
and my heart
tendering not the honey
that runs from between my legs
at a moment's calling
but my love

and if it's not the rope you need
to climb that mountain
not small feathers under your wings
that lift you up
not the bulletproof vest
to ward off assassination

forgive me
forgive me my inadequacy

i have nothing to offer
but a love that lasts forever
take some please
perhaps it will moisten your tongue
cool your throat
coat a corner of a not-yet-full belly
perhaps it will
soothe your heart

forgive my paucity
i have nothing to offer
but my love

During my tenure as poet laureate I will make every effort to give voice to more poets and poetry, and to let the poets and the poems demonstrate poetry's capacity to heal, to give vision, to provide clarity, and to offer love. It is indeed a privilege and an honor to have this opportunity to serve as Poet Laureate of San Francisco. Once again, I thank you.

devorah major
April 30, 2002

poetry is breath, blood, bone,
scriptures, curses, rhythm vowels
angles, curves and purpose.

poetry teacher

lately i am too full of lessons
fuses in one hand
matches in the other
discreet little sacks of
gunpowder under my tongue

explode a poem
a poem of fireworks
a noisy poem
a poem that burns your fingers
and makes your eyes water

i have poems crumpled
in the bottom of my purse
poems used as bookmarks in
anthologies of poems

poems on the back of bookmarks
poems on the front of bookmarks
lessons on bookmark poems
short lines
few words
special typeface

so many lessons
how to write a poem on nothing

how to write a poem when it runs away from you
how to write a poem that tastes good
how to write a poem that smells funny
how to write a funny poem
how to make fun of a poem

i have so many lessons
cut words
add details
use texture
seek simplicity
be real
imagine the impossible
growl

turn into a poem
turn a poem into you
i am a teacher of poetry
a guide through contradictions
make yr poem
now make it disappear
the poem lives
in that flash
between becoming and dissolving

black lit class
and ellison's invisible man

for dr. raye richardson

0.

raye   said, zero is an abstract
condition that exists
only on a theoretical plane

where is there nothing

there may be no chair
there may be no people
there may be no oxygen
but there is never nothing

zero is only a thought
even in the void
that emptiness that is
eternal and never ending
that gave birth
to the something that is
us and our universe

even in that place

without light
without sound
without breath
that place all people speak of
when they look back
to the beginnings
seeking the thread
of the first ancestor
trying to replant the
impossible memory
of the time
before we were born
of a thought
found in the middle of the void
even there
zero
is only a mathematical ideal
and even if the first ones were birthed from it
we no longer hold anything of that place
except a certain fear of loneliness
that haunts our memory
and the paradox of something
existing inside of nothing

1.

raye   continued, one
is only an assumption.
one is a particular point of view
that does not always represent a total
understanding of the complexity of unity.
it, like zero, makes counting much easier.

but
look under a microscope at the one
and it immediately becomes many
one human, many cells
many worlds
producing
reproducing
living
dying
so many bound and held together
by the assumption of one

2.

which brings us to invisible
invisible pretends at zero
exists as one
and always seems to imply
no less than two

invisible usually means only
unseen by another

invisible exists only if
it is comprised of one who is not seen
and one who does not see

3.

reading literature
learning mathematics
seeking god

a red love poem

it is the abstraction of words that continues to confound me.
r-e-d is not red. or vermilion. or scarlet.
it doesn't drip
it isn't flush with heat
there is no glow.
r-e-d are three letters pressed on a page.
rouge. maroon. sangria.
there is no flavor
no scent
no color.
r-e-d represents, but is not, itself.

red, no less or more a word than love.
i smile in you. run my fingers
down the side of your face.
taste your lips.
your heart turns toward me. hears.

but here on the page. love does not love.
it is not the act. only a heading for a chapter.
there is no size. no weight,
no movement to this love.
it indicates, but does not become.

words are thought stilled. but thought is never still
thoughts are caught and then they slip away

or hover and then dig deeper in
thought frightens surprises impels compels.
thought is never still.
but words are held static
by the edges of the page.
frozen on a flat white tundra.

still
i love you
scarlet
vermilion
sangria
red.

i grow my poems

"Poetry ought to have a mother as well as a father."
— George Eliot

i grow my poems
where i grow my babies
they gestate and are birthed
some prematurely
some late term
some sliding out easily

most come
with long labors
during the dark
crevices of morning

occasionally breech
sometimes deformed
usually wailing

to be sure
when it comes to poems
i have lain with enough
to not be sure who
the father of each one is
when a father is
if a father is

but i am a mother true
and my poems
like my children of flesh
crowd my dreams
my room
my laughter
my fear

contest format

slammed words rush into the mike
screeched passion scared image vote

screeched passion scared image vote
fractioned performance tepid score

fractioned performance tepid score
where's the poet with truth's song

slammed words rush into the mike

writing workshops with the homeless

steve writes
"i want to write
i want to write
i want to write"

john says a poetry critic
lives inside his elbow
jumping to shoulder and then ear
where he shouts insults devoid
of any scrap of advice

rose says she never can write
in a workshop setting
and then fills pages and pages
with words

ezra says he can only write
about the war
darryl says he can only write
in abstractions

marvelle makes up words
as she writes her fragmented thoughts
fitting them together like
mismatched parts of broken vases

who of them is ready
to pull apart their ribcage
cradle their heart
investigate the scars and
clogged memories
wrapped in thorns

peanut flirts with me
"can i make you smile
if i give you a poem"

walter jumps up and down
holding one line and one
line only from kamau da'ood

"if you can see it, you can be it
if you can see it, you can be it"
then runs from the room
only to return quoting the line again
"if you can see it, you can be it"
before he runs away again

cynthia creates mirrors of herself
then breaks them
and hides the pieces in her pockets
her hands bleed and when we notice
she accuses us of trying to sever her veins

i feed them pastries and poems

coffee and history
stale ghirardelli chocolate
and pep-squad cheers

i pretend i know
how to teach writing
notice this, i say
practice that, i advise
image
      detail

              precision
              create form
              defy structure

              but it's all a lie

              jump off a cliff
              i should tell them

run around naked
in a field full of strangers

try to fly without wings

speak a language
you never learned
without using your tongue

die again and again

don't sleep
do not whatever you do
fall asleep into the valley
of endless dream sestinas
repeating end words
disappearing with each scene change

chew on some razor blades
walk on some burning coals

you say you want to write
fuck a friend instead
then bask in the afterglow
it's a lot more fun

you say you want to write
fuck yourself

i don't know
how to teach writing
only fools and crazy people
lovers and politicians want to write

let me show you how to make a pie crust
the trick is to handle it as little as possible
balance the butter to flour so that the mixture
fluffs in the bowl
roll it out gently with an even hand

don't write
cook
it tempts the nostrils
fills the belly and does
wonders for the heart

oh, did i mention
brown sugar for the filling?

first person singular

i find my use of "i" in poems enters and recedes in waves that sometimes last years. it seems that i spent the last year using first person singular more than i have in quite some time. my poems wore "i" in many forms, as self, and as voice of other(s). then too, i have been reading and noticing the contexts of "i" in the work of others. and i have been questioning its role.

> it is true we have no right to assume that the "i" in a poem is the poet; only that the poet has tried to get to the core of a particular voice, moment, truth to reveal a certain color from the inside.

but does the poet have a responsibility to say, "this i is me, but this i is the voice of another?" or, "this is my story, but, this is a truth i have learned by surveying, but not walking in, an other's proverbial shoes?"

> what is our obligation to truth of self in this equation, or does it matter? is this revealing of the "i" in a poem merely filling a prurient interest, or a pornographic ideal that demands full front photographs legs spread genitalia revealed, skin blemishes untouched?

> is it enough to simply rest in the clarity of the i of the poem, and not press to know that the i was poet-self, or relative, or friend, or a person seen once, as a lightning flash on a dimly lit corner?

are we safe to say the i is always our self, like an actor who effectively plays corruption or deceit by finding their fertile seeds in her own heart? all emotions and potentialities are in us, so, i and i is, in truth, always the case.

is it that universal truth of oneness that this undisclosed i reaches for?

or is there something in the self
the "i" revealed, that is a central part of the poem?
in whatever universe the poem navigates through
does it travel from the openness of that i?
from the reflection of that i?
from a *look at me, no arms* calling of one's own name?

and what of the reader? do we write for only the ideal reader? the one who brings no assumptions, but somehow carries a depth of experience to the work? do we worry about the others who are not clear if it is or is not the poet who lives inside the i? or does it matter again? isn't it only important that the reader believe it was someone's truth? does not the i become them, just as much as the directive you can be both reader and writer? in a good reading of the poem doesn't the reader take the voice of "i" and live some moments, some minutes, some curves and angles inside the poem's persona, invented or concealed? and doesn't this experience make the actuality of "i" little more than a gossip columnist's item, or a historical sidebar footnote that only points up the truth, or missed truth, already evidenced in the poem?

when, if ever, does it matter
if the i is self or the i is mirror?

i am asking this question.
me the writer. me the reader.

i am asking it of you.

political poem

what makes a poem revolutionary
does it violently refuse the page
construct a chaos of grammar
that denies metaphor or defeats meter
is it armed and ready for prolonged struggle
is it loud and insistent assaulting your senses
full of gun powder and iron pellets
is it unavailable for canonization
despite an early death as martyr
or does it instead
find guerrilla survival
hidden
underground
exploding in unexpected places
appearing once again   just
when you thought it dead

a cuba song

they say we are lost   guanhatabey
that no one knows our name   guanhatabey

but we are the thread that hold the beads
of this old cuba that becomes home to all travelers

we are the thread that holds the beads of this new cuba
where flamenco collides with rhumba

this new cuba that waits for fresh water
and pleads for fresh fruits
prays for soap to remember the baths
which our cousins made famous   cibones
and our cousins made prayer   taino
we are the thread that holds the beads

this new cuba is not of our making
but we had lain with the spanish
and shaped the fingertips of their flamenco
we had lain with the africans
and our feet embraced the earth between our toes
as they wedded rhumba

we too knew the drum and the circle
the dance and the prayer
we were and will be again   guanhatabey

each truckload who comes to worship in the cemeteries
brings baskets of their gods with them
carries them on their shoulders and in their mouths

elegua, they bow as they enter the crossroads
obatala, they chant as they prepare the doves
oshun, they whisper trembling in their hips
jesus, they weep recalling nails and blood
so many gods, so many names

these new ones light candles and make sacrifice
cross themselves and supplicate

but we are still here hidden in a corner of their hearts

the first people to know this land
people of the sweet fruit and sea shell

it was we who named her cuba.
and when they dance we dance with them   guanhatabey.

they say we are lost   guanhatabey
but we are the string that holds the beads and remembers
how we knit our songs and wove our dances and called our home
cuba cuba cuba

aliens

we are all aliens
traveling in outer space

only a few of the first ones stayed
nestled beneath mount kilimanjaro
in the belly of our ancestors' birthing
on the lips our mother's womb

all of the rest of us
have forebears
who walked or rode
to come to where we now reside

all of the rest of us have traveled
to here where our heads lie
and where our children
grow or wither or perish

all were natives before the ones
whose names we have forgotten
began their trek
all were natives
before the ones who stayed
stopped telling stories of we who had left

eons ago we had no questions

about who was our kin
everyone was related to us

then we began to travel
turned each the other
into opposites
becoming and creating
aliens

2.
we aliens travel
through our dark milky galaxy
circling a sun ghosted by a moon
orbiting in concert with no less than eight planets

and as we travel with and without each other
we sometimes meet meteors
that whistle through stardust
creating craters
shaping sandstorms
digging lake beds
raining mineral deposits
seeded with fossilized amoebas

and as we travel with and without each other
comets sail by hot smoky ice tails shimmering

and as we pass comet moving past us
we see stars fall from the sky and marvel

at being in the middle of all these galactic wonders

everywhere we go we are traveling with and as
aliens in outer space on this planet where we live

and everywhere we stay
we are surrounded by other voyagers
like and unlike us

i know
i've always been an outsider
amidst immigrants
beside aliens
next to strangers
just like you

on continuing to struggle

for Mumia Abu Jamal

i don't want to write a memorial poem
in commemoration of the fact
that another knot was tied in
our tongues

i don't want to write a *we gave more blood*
to water their poison crops poem
the *on reviewing the execution*
of another black man poem

a man who could see through cells without windows
who could speak though bound and gagged
who could lead under chain behind bars
from isolated chambers
while penned in a land where
as a matter of policy
family is forbidden to touch
except through glass

who of us could hold our heart intact
who of us could keep the vision so strong
that others become bright in its glow

i do not want to write
a *we tried but ain't it a shame* poem
a *what a god damn crime* poem
a *we did all we could, but still* poem
a *they won this round*
we'll have to get them the next time poem
a *lost more than ground this time* poem
a *they killed him anyway* poem
a *we didn't stop them* poem

i'm not going to carry banners of defeat
and wear shackles of resignation
i say i want to sing praises in celebration
not through mourning
i say i want to give thanks for community
that is birthing new freedoms
not burying fresh kill

i'm going to work on a *the road is long but we still truckin'* poem
going to work on a *keep scaling that mountain* poem
going to work on a *making sure there are better days ahead* poem
working on a *free mumia* poem
working on freeing mumia
working on seeing mumia free

july ritual

firecrackers gunshots quiet
still night thinned by summer fog

still night thinned by summer fog
check all doors lock curtained windows

check all doors lock curtained windows
sleep hides under empty bed

firecrackers gunshots quiet

august has always been black for us

we are born every month
in every month we die
each month has some triumphs
and each carries its own defeats

but august
august has always been black for us
black august since those first twenty
landed in 1619 jamestown
and felt its wet hungry
lash cut their sturdy backs
as they discovered how deeply
shackles could cleave

that first twenty
of millions who would
drown or slave
and did not know
how many centuries
spirit, flesh, and soul
would stay bound
by the scars
from that august arrival

we remember nat turner
we hold onto george jackson

we do not forget his brother jonathan
and the others who fell and fall
warriors reaching for freedom

a MOVE house flooded
burned and crushed
that philadelphia august day
and august night when watts exploded
black reflecting on a fire sky

we've known this month
for nearly four hundred years
we know this august

this august that has
always been
black
for us

sign post

colored water
quarter water
purple water
sugar

still water
deep water
salt water
river

clear water
ice water
rain water
hailing

break water
hard water
white water
drown

terrorism defined

1.
i was a child
when i first saw the pictures
black men's bodies
hanging from trees

castrated
burnt
picnic
laughed
the men and women
with their children

nigger cookout
some of them seemed to speak
into the camera lens
the smell of burnt flesh
fresh in their nostrils

i've been against terrorism
for a long time

2.
as a teen read pieces of the rise and fall
of the third reich
not much more than a footnote

the points on jewish flesh stretched into lampshades
which, as it happened, echoed the fate of
slave rebellion leader nat turner
a hundred years earlier
when his lush-hued skin was cut and dried
and then fashioned into a purse and
a never-quite-translucent lamp shade
displayed in his captor's home

i've been against terrorism
for a long time

stood and marched
as vietnam warriors
would come and go leaving
chemical forests, massive graves
and skulls presaging
cambodian death trails

over half a million iraqi children are dead
the first from bombs and poisoned water
then more from plutonium poisoning
disease and starvation

every thirty days thirty-five hundred young people
waste away as if someone were blowing up
a child-full world trade center
inside iraq every single month

and now america cries
speaks mournfully of mothers
who could not come home from work
fathers who had houses and dreams
turned to bone ash that got caught in our
phlegm-filled lungs and tear-spilling eyes
and yes we cry
for the losses of all of those
who were loved
who are loved
who are bombed
who were incinerated
who came to rest under hundreds of tons
of concrete and iron
plaster and glass
in barbarous acts
like so many others
that i have lived under
that i have seen grow

terrorism that's personal
a man dragged behind a truck
until his arm is pulled from socket
his leg torn from hip
his head sawed from neck

terrorism that's intimate
a woman raped invaded assaulted
beaten bruised broken

by men strangers and lovers
family every twelve seconds

terrorism that's official
a night stick pushed up a black man's anus
as a station full of police turn their heads
ignore the screams
a west african immigrant shot at 42 times
until 19 bullets make him
crumble in his own doorway
while trying to show his papers

terrorism that's global
i have lost my mother my father
my brother my sister my hope
i have lost my family
so i have lost my hope
cries a man who speaks
after the bombing of his
afghani village
as the terrorists advance
boldly waving their flags

4.
america i hear you sing that
liberty is your mother
is it daddy then who rapes
because america
it is you who feeds

this monster its largest meals
you who stokes its hottest fires

no
you are not alone
and no
you were not the first
but now america you
set the standard
look at the people you have killed
start anywhere in your history
any day
the first days
this morning
spin a globe in your hand
and look where your armies live
look where they draw weapons
look where their armaments are used

but as for this american-born woman
grown strong and free inside
your rotting belly
america
terrorism has been a regular part of my world
all my life and i have been fighting it
long as i can remember
saying no as loud as i knew how

no pledges needed

no waving flags required
no uniformed allegiance
recited with bandaged mouths
necks gripped
until one can barely breathe
let me state it clearly again and again
i've been against terrorism
for a long time
been
against terrorism
against all terrorism

against terrorism
against all terrorism

against terrorism
against all terrorism for forever

to bomb

as the terrorists who taught the terrorists
as the terrorists who arm the terrorists
as the terrorists who show themselves
to be the terrorists of all terrorists
proclaim that they will bombard
assert that they will barrage
assure that they will bomb
and bomb and bomb
until there are no other
terrorists to bomb

we should remember
that to bomb is
to be bankrupt
to be deficient
to bomb is
to flail
to fizzle
to flop
to be defeated through one's own actions

peace negotiation

what would our world be
if together we all agreed
to make women's genitalia
sacrosanct once again

if there were no rapes
if there were no beatings
if there was no violation
if there was no cut no gash
no laceration

if all that came forth sugar juices
tissue full blood from the womb
through the vagina
past the labia
under the clitoris
if all of that was treated
as a blessing
instead of a curse

dark love

sleep visions of him
as he sits alone on sharp stairs
turns from the frozen salt
that digs a path across his cheek
pouring out a sadness

i taste it on my tongue
feel it burn acid
grit
tar
marking lines passed
generation to generation
bleeding deeply with each chain link
a well-guarded secret
this tear that never dries

our sweat meshes
his arms unfold
pull me inward
past all mirages
past frozen walls of rage
past survivals many doors
the tear curtains/pain broken songs
endless dreams tied up with roach egg casings
pulled past ancestor screams
demands for reparations

urging us to avenge their loss
harsh screeches inside our brains
taunting, pleading, chanting
to free them, us
sorrow people moaning/dark warm/moaning
drawing lines into his face

holding tight he pushes me on
through the white wall, refined
purified, salt, sugar white
a light so bright it burns
holes in our eye sockets
white ash/a film on the tongue
covering mornings awakenings
the cold of the poles
snowed-in/infinitely silent
tomb-stiff/the color of death

night visions
the turning away
the tears no man is supposed to cry
tears from the womb
dark tears pouring from him
engraved, cheek lined, deep tears
pushed into windowless jail cells
smelling of urine brine
tears from when he was left alone
once again, to reconsider death

slave ship memories/buried deep in tears
crouched plantation begging layered on top
weeping from a spirit too long lashed
to bars, stretched twisted tears
from when we were babies black
and learned the difference
as pale hands reached out to feel innocent heads
grease rubbed blood fingers into short soft curls
spat and made a nigger wish.

tears, learning a new kind of darkness
forgetting too soon
the beauty of his mother's womb
dark blues learnt and sung
didn't he know the words by heart
as his mother hummed gray cold mornings
as his father beat them thick to form another overcoat
trying to protect him from the ice of enduring winter
that was the only promise given

he pulls me through the morass
tears burning on his cheek
as if i cannot see them/touch them.
he pulls hard, until i am warm
inside his tenderness, behind the bloodied curtains
resting in jeweled darkness

endless plant earth warm around me
tender as a touch/tender as a dream

through the maze he brought me here
to this place from where his seeds spring
this place where all skin is smooth and pliant
dark as the beat of the kuumba drum
timeless beyond tears in this hidden valley
where guarded he keeps his soul

tender/fragile quiet he sings
a song from before the priest of voodoo
made of our hearts a system of love
guarded with candle-lit mazes
burning black warding off terror
a song he sings from before
folded layers of madness
cloaks of taut survival

a song quiet he sings
as he woos me back to sleep
promises full sun at daybreak
so i can lay naked/warm my belly
swollen full of life

he holds me close, inside
assured that no enemies
will slip in and disturb our rest

he sings a song
from when time began
soft, into my ear he sings

to sweeten dreams

i lay against the cushion of his soul
as demons rain about me
safe/i listen, dream
and feel the child grow

tendered love

i give this to you
who are young
and beautiful
take this
to your children:
dream

dream
of telling your children
of the days when you were young
and crack and ice were spread
across your streets

dream of talking
with your children's children
about the days when you could chill
as long as it didn't get too cold

about how winter set deep and hard
on you and your friends

about how sometimes you forgot who
your friends were

about how some of your friends
forgot themselves

about how you remembered
and survived

dream of telling them
about the white snow queens
who chased you down the streets

about how slavers took freddie cougar
and jason and all their other
won't-die-bogeymen-ghouls
and mixed in a little rock
that would make a baby forget its mama
and a man cut out his heart
just to suck and blow
and taste that smoke

dream of being alive
to tell them
about the days when some
fought over the shade of a jacket
the line of a running shoe
the stitches in a jeans back pocket
the days when you couldn't even look
at somebody unless you were ready
to come on up or back on down

dream of being able to tell them
of the days when death slept

at the foot of your bed
rising to stalk your streets

dream of telling them about
you warrior strong
how you fought
came up from inside singing
me
i
am
no slave
will wear
no chains
i'm rich and ancient
i want to live long
and free

dream of being able
to tell them
how you saw it differently
and grabbed onto everyone nearby
who saw it differently too
and together demanded
a better future

together made a path for each other
together made a path for your children
and your children's children

and as you lean over those babies
and feel their little arms
hot and close
remember being young

and tell them again and again

how you had to
battle out the fog
to sing your song and
help your sun to rise

how you started from inside
and found courage
looked through clear sharp eyes
and saw the choices
to give your children
to gift your grandchildren
this which i give
love full to you

a future to turn
into a wonder.
start in
the links you can forge
friend to friend.
cover each other's back
turn again into family
make allies of all those

who would be free

refuse to be overseer
whipping your sister
refuse to be lash
on the back of your brother
for a color he wears
for a music she hears
for a crimp in their walk
for a style in their talk

remember
you are
no slaves
will wear
no chains
are dark
and rich
and ancient.

you can have all
the tomorrows you want
alive and dancing
take them
make them
yours
together

catch

on masks

i find it hard to breathe
inside a mask
my face immediately
begins to sweat
my nose to itch
my cheeks to chafe

yet how beautiful
they are who wear masks well
revealing a hidden essence
under the guise of artifice

how beautiful they are
who become the mask
awaken an ancient song
and help its spirit dance

but as for me
i keep my mask inside
eyes closed
sealing the mouth
of my heart

untitled ancestry

i a mongrel
a crossbreed
a mutt
a grafting of cultures
a planet varied
sea to land
calm to storm
wondering in the mirror
where did the eyes come from
and the texture of hair
who saw to the skin tones
and who to the lips
arbitrarily naming the source
of my limbs
my hips
my face
i landless
homeless
being so much a mixture
a couscous of spices and fruits

a mongrel of the comings together
chosen/forced of so many different ones
a crossbreed that fills the spaces
between rich dark and translucent fair
a mutt that has unruly fur

cropping out in varied shades
ears and tail being strangely incongruent

i the grafting of cultures
that insists where love fails
life will persist, thrive, recreate
a planet varied mountains to hills
to valleys to chasms deep
waterfalls to rivers to streams
to oceans wide a melange i
claiming space on the rainbow.

in answer

gypsy they whisper as sallow curse
negrita they spit as if black was not
the color that gives birth to the stars

my skin glows with the shadows
of their gods and when i dance
all of our ancestors smile
as i remember them and know
my home is wherever
my feet and my heart embrace

queen of hearts

i harvest hearts
don't steal them
don't buy them
just gather them like
dandelion blossoms
then turn the seeds to wine

i collect hearts
one at a time
each selected for its
size and shape and cadence
i let them go unwillingly
and never before i have
engraved my initials deeply
inside the rim

on speaking of lonely

i am daughter to lonely
lover
friend
confidante even

some nights we spar until
i pass out from its lightning
crosscuts
left jab to the chin
right uppercut to the belly

i eat the bitter of lonely
bathe in its sea-green waters
dance to its wordless song
sleep in its unlit cave

it no longer chases me
down crowded streets
or trips me up at dinner parties

i have surrendered to its will
and welcome the familiarity
of its dry, silent touch

privacy

privacy in thought or deed
is sold as ugly now,
something suspect
probably immoral.
in these cable, video,
satellite-hooked up-to-the-minute
24/7 newsy days a year,
privacy has become
a grunt in the army
of no distinction.
the sordid secret
off-color, slanted, unknown fact
about which others insinuate
and sneer offering too much concern
for the subject of what goes on
behind your shades
under your covers
in the back of your closed doors
in the corners of your mind
which is to say in private
if not always alone.
so privacy has had to go
somewhere else to live
reaching the end and start
of its cycle at the same time.
a lone tone breathed into the sunset

the whistle of collapsing foam
the quiet splendor of privacy
looking for a shelter
in the well space of your palm
and the darkness of your laugh.

error in time

i have been wrong about time
once thought it had substance

thought i could count it
as it rambled by
sheep
pennies
days

thought i could wear it
even taste it
bitter
saccharin
sizzling
nectar deep in the bowl of my tongue
seasoned gristle chewed
into minutes
seconds
microseconds
until i found myself
eating more of it
but enjoying less
as i would divide dissect defy
and of course at times be defeated
by time's machinations

i was wrong about time
until i realized that time
was a man-made invention
a dark-cloaked figure
scythe poised
to cut us down
never enough
always too much
need more
can't catch it
fast as we race
can't catch it
always in front of us
and in back
always on top of us
and underneath

it was weighing me down
until universal time was declared
and a logarithm for new time
conversions was created
a virtual time for a virtual world
inside the actual world
where we all live

time hacked into
binary lines and angles
until we all fit into the same moment
so when the sun creeps up kilimanjaro

and the moon settles over mauna loa
and a lizard is wedged between rock shadows
in the flatlands of the painted desert
we can name it all the same moment in
computer-synched universal time

i watch
time definitely and infinitely fall
into the plethora of violence
and the paucity of healing
that is the stopwatch
of our era

i know time
as contracts we keep
or break with each other
with ourselves
a memory we smell or forget
a terror we confront or duck
a bridge we blow up
or build

i had been wrong in thinking
time moved
when it was the earth that shook
the sky that rushed
we that surged

i had been wrong

in believing that times change
when it was the world that changes
as we nourish or reduce
the life around us

we through our growth and decay
have always invented
and continue to invent
that god-like entity
which we call time

amends

have i told you
that i love words
that i embrace them as my constant lover
am always available early dawns
rain-filled evenings
midnight moonrises
or when sun burns her way
through the midday fog   always
paying heed to their insistent call
melting like warm honey
when they put their fire
to my fingers
to my tongue

have i told you i loved words

then i have lied
for i love them true
but not all the time

sometimes it is only an
aimless flirtation
a distraction from fast-food television
something to do when the floorboards creaked
and night's thickness made me tremble
a hermit's plaything

an isolate's reason
a litany chanted in a room of fun-house mirrors
a ritual of form complete with holy water and incense

forgive me for all my betrayals

i have spit words out as so much phlegm
laced with strands of blood
i have squandered words in gutters
washed them down sewers
treated them as waste
to be buried or burnt

i have shredded words
until they became scraps
crowding the corners of my room
falling in confetti piles around my ankles
needing only to be swept away
i have turned my back and ignored them
called them shallow and flat
forsaken them
declared that only
music could speak to me
and then refused to listen

i have sat with nursery rhymes
circling my skull
and made praise of doggerel

i have taken words for granted
scraped them like mud on the
mat i use to wipe my feet

i have shown words my disrespect
left them like flavorless gum
on the bottom of my desk

forgive me all my betrayals

it is not the words' fault
they have done only
what i have asked

if they cowered in corners
it is because i beat them
if they winced and then splintered
at awkward angles
it is because i screeched
denied them their truths
and muffled their rhythms

if they hid until
they became faint with hunger
it is because i called them whore
became a pimp and secured tricks
in high-rise buildings
with elevators that went only
from basement to roof and back

to basement again

i have betrayed words
forgive me

it was not love
but obsession
the need to control
to manage
and have dominion
over chaos
it was habit and addiction
it was greed

so they abandoned me
just got up and walked
like a cuckolded spouse
cleaned out the house
took all the furniture
cut off the phone
and left no note

i begged them to come back
sent them scented notes
and expensive gifts
prayed and fasted
admitted all my sins
until they returned
calling the shots

making me climb
from beneath thick downy comforter
to be chilled in the morning's night
lifting me out of a steaming bath
to leave puddles of bubbles
and the scent of lavender
as a trail across the floor

again i pull my car to the shoulder of the road
write notes on the bottoms of tissue boxes
phrases on newspaper margins

the words are laughing at me
but they stay now
as long as i treat them kindly
as long as i love them truly

and i do love them

have i told you i need words
that they are my cornbread and greens
my summer melons and winter yams

though i have been unfaithful
again i love them true

firefly and star
incandescent embers
we shining human

devorah major is a poet, novelist, and essayist who has published prize-winning works of fiction and poetry. Among her books are *Open Weave, Brown Glass Windows,* and *street smarts.* She lives in San Francisco, where she works as an editor and arts administrator.

CITY LIGHTS FOUNDATION is a nonprofit foundation that supports literacy and the literary arts.

All contributions are gratefully accepted and fully tax deductible.

261 Columbus Avenue
San Francisco California 94133
www.citylights.com
staff@citylights.com